Being Prepared

The Key to Unlocking Success

The Importance of Preparation to Seize Opportunities

Gerard Assey

Being Prepared

The Key to Unlocking Success

By

Gerard Assey

Published by:

Gerard Assey

19/18, Palli Arasan Street

Anna Nagar East

Chennai - 600 102

ISBN: 978-81-971121-9-5

(Image courtesy Freepik: www.Freepik.com-Thank You)

Table of Contents

Preface

Welcome to **'Being Prepared: The Key to Unlocking Success** *(The Importance of Preparation to Seize Opportunities).*

This book is a comprehensive guide to the importance of preparation in achieving success in all aspects of life. Whether you are striving for personal growth, professional advancement, or seeking to seize opportunities, being prepared is the key that unlocks your potential.

In these pages, you will find a wealth of information, insights, and practical strategies to help you enhance your preparedness and seize opportunities. We will explore the significance of preparation, the benefits it offers, and the repercussions of not being prepared. Through real-life examples, expert advice, and actionable steps, you will learn how to develop a mindset and lifestyle that prioritize readiness and resilience.

Each chapter is designed to provide you with valuable insights and tools that you can apply to your own life. From understanding the importance of preparation to learning how to avoid over-preparing, this book offers a comprehensive approach to preparing for success.

As you embark on this journey, I encourage you to approach each chapter with an open mind and a willingness to learn. The principles and strategies outlined in this book have the power to transform your life and unlock your full potential. By embracing the importance of preparation, you are taking the first step toward a more successful and fulfilling future.

I hope that this book serves as a valuable resource and inspires you to embrace preparation as a lifelong companion on your journey to success.

Best wishes on your journey to being prepared and unlocking your success.

Why a Book on Preparation?

In a world filled with uncertainties and challenges, preparation serves as a guiding light that illuminates our path towards success. Preparation can be defined as the process of getting ready for a specific event or situation by making plans, acquiring knowledge, and developing skills. It is not merely a task to check off a list but rather a mindset that shapes our approach to life's opportunities and challenges.

Importance of Preparation in Personal and Professional Life

Preparation plays a crucial role in both personal and professional spheres. In our personal lives, being prepared enables us to handle unexpected events with grace and composure. Whether it's preparing for a family gathering, a vacation, or a personal project, being prepared allows us to enjoy these moments more fully and reduces stress and anxiety.

In the professional realm, preparation is the key to achieving success and advancing in one's career. Whether it's preparing for a job interview, a presentation, or a business meeting, being well-prepared instills confidence and increases the likelihood of favorable outcomes. Moreover, preparation demonstrates professionalism and a commitment to excellence, traits that are highly valued in any professional setting.

Overview of the Book's Structure

This book is structured to provide a comprehensive guide to the art of preparation. Each chapter is

designed to explore different aspects of preparation, from its importance and benefits to practical strategies and real-life examples. By the end of this book, readers will have gained a deeper understanding of the role preparation plays in their lives and will have acquired the tools necessary to embrace preparation as a cornerstone of their success.
Throughout the chapters, readers will encounter stories of individuals who have achieved remarkable success through careful preparation. These real-life examples serve as inspiration and illustrate the transformative power of preparation. Additionally, each chapter includes practical tips and exercises to help readers apply the principles of preparation to their own lives.

In essence, this book is a roadmap to unlocking the potential that lies within each of us. It is a testament to the power of preparation and a call to action for readers to embrace preparation as a lifelong pursuit. By doing so, they will not only seize the opportunities that come their way but also navigate the challenges of life with confidence and resilience.

Why is Preparation Important?

In our journey through life, preparation is the silent force that shapes our destiny. It is the meticulous planning, the thoughtful consideration, and the deliberate action that pave the way for our success. Preparation is not just a means to an end; it is the very foundation upon which our goals are built and achieved.

Significance of Preparation in Achieving Goals

Preparation is the bridge that connects our aspirations to reality. Without it, our goals remain distant dreams, unattainable and out of reach. Whether we aspire to climb the corporate ladder, start a business, or achieve personal milestones, preparation is the key that unlocks these possibilities. Consider, for example, the story of Thomas Edison, the inventor of the light bulb. Edison famously said, "Genius is one percent inspiration and ninety-nine percent perspiration." His success was not merely a stroke of luck or a moment of brilliance; it was the result of years of painstaking preparation, countless experiments, and relentless dedication to his vision.

How Preparation Sets the Foundation for Success

Preparation is not just about being ready for the expected; it is about being ready for the unexpected. It is about anticipating challenges, devising strategies, and having the resilience to overcome obstacles. In essence, preparation is about being proactive rather than reactive, about taking control of our destiny rather than leaving it to chance.

Take, for instance, the story of Serena Williams, one of the greatest tennis players of all time. Williams didn't become a champion overnight; her success was the result of years of rigorous training, disciplined practice, and mental preparation. She didn't just show up on the court and hope for the best; she prepared herself physically, mentally, and emotionally, giving herself the best possible chance to succeed.

Examples of Successful Individuals Who Attribute Their Achievements to Preparation

Countless successful individuals attribute their achievements to preparation. From athletes to entrepreneurs, from artists to scientists, the common thread that binds them is their unwavering commitment to preparation. They understand that success is not a matter of luck or talent alone; it is a result of meticulous planning, relentless effort, and unwavering determination.

Consider the example of Oprah Winfrey, a media mogul, and philanthropist. Winfrey didn't become one of the most influential women in the world by chance; her success was the result of careful planning, hard work, and a steadfast belief in herself. She once said, "I believe luck is preparation meeting opportunity. If you hadn't been prepared when the opportunity came along, you wouldn't have been lucky."

In conclusion, preparation is not just a habit; it is a mindset. It is about approaching life with intentionality, purpose, and foresight. It is about taking the time to prepare ourselves for the challenges and opportunities that lie ahead, knowing that our success depends on it. As we embark on this journey of exploration and discovery, let us remember that preparation is not a burden but a blessing, a gift we give ourselves to live our best lives and achieve our greatest potential.

Reflection Questions: Why is Preparation Important?

- ✓ How has lack of preparation impacted your past experiences or opportunities?
- ✓ What are some areas of your life where you could benefit from better preparation?
- ✓ How can you prioritize preparation in your daily routine to enhance your overall success?

Benefits of Being Prepared

Preparation is not just a task we undertake to achieve a specific goal; it is a mindset that has far-reaching benefits in all aspects of our lives. In this chapter, we will explore the various benefits of being prepared, from increased confidence and better decision-making to higher success rates in our endeavors.

1. Increased Confidence:

One of the most noticeable benefits of being prepared is the increase in confidence it brings. When we are well-prepared, we approach challenges with a sense of assurance, knowing that we have done our homework and are ready to face whatever comes our way. This confidence is not just a psychological boost; it also translates into tangible results, as others are more likely to trust and follow someone who exudes confidence.

Being prepared boosts confidence levels, as you approach tasks and challenges knowing that you are well-equipped to handle them.

2. Better Decision-Making:

Preparation also leads to better decision-making. When we take the time to gather information, analyze options, and consider possible outcomes, we are able to make more informed decisions. This not only increases the likelihood of a positive outcome but also reduces the risk of making hasty or ill-informed decisions that can have negative consequences.

Preparation allows for more informed decision-making, as you have considered various options and their potential outcomes.

3. Higher Success Rates:

Perhaps the most compelling benefit of being prepared is the higher success rates it brings. Whether in business, education, sports, or any other endeavor, those who are well-prepared are more likely to achieve their goals and succeed in their pursuits. This is because preparation not only increases our chances of success but also allows us to make the most of the opportunities that come our way.

Those who are prepared are more likely to succeed, as they are able to seize opportunities and overcome obstacles more effectively.

4. Reduced Stress:

Preparation reduces stress by minimizing last-minute scrambling and uncertainties, leading to a more relaxed and focused mindset.

5. Improved Time Management:

Being prepared helps in managing time more effectively, as you are able to prioritize tasks and allocate resources efficiently.

6. Enhanced Performance:

Preparation leads to improved performance, as you are able to showcase your skills and abilities more effectively.

7. Increased Productivity:

Preparedness leads to increased productivity, as you are able to accomplish more in less time with greater efficiency.

8. Greater Resilience:

Being prepared enhances resilience, as you are better able to adapt to unexpected challenges and setbacks.

9. Improved Relationships:

Preparation fosters better relationships, as others appreciate your reliability and ability to follow through on commitments.

10. Personal Growth:

Finally, being prepared facilitates personal growth, as you continually challenge yourself and strive for improvement.

Real-Life Examples

To illustrate the benefits of being prepared, let us consider the story of Steve Jobs, the co-founder of Apple Inc. Jobs was known for his meticulous preparation and attention to detail, traits that played a significant role in his success. From product launches to keynote presentations, Jobs was always well-prepared, and this preparation contributed to Apple's success as a company.

Another example is that of J.K. Rowling, the author of the Harry Potter series. Before writing the first book in the series, Rowling spent years planning and outlining the entire seven-book series. This preparation not only helped her stay focused and organized but also ensured that the story had a cohesive and compelling narrative arc, leading to its immense success.

In conclusion, the benefits of being prepared are manifold and far-reaching. From increased confidence and better decision-making to higher success rates, preparation is the key that unlocks our full potential and allows us to achieve our goals. By embracing preparation as a way of life, we can navigate life's challenges with ease and confidence, knowing that we are fully equipped to seize the opportunities that come our way.

Reflection Questions: Benefits of Being Prepared

- ✓ Reflect on a time when being prepared positively impacted an outcome in your life. What benefits did you experience?
- ✓ How do you think increased confidence from being prepared can influence your decision-making?
- ✓ What steps can you take to improve your decision-making skills through better preparation?

Reasons Why Preparation is Crucial

Preparation is not just a habit; it is a mindset that can make the difference between success and failure. In this chapter, we will explore ten compelling reasons why preparation is crucial in both personal and professional life, supported by anecdotes and studies that highlight its significance.

1. Anticipation of Challenges:

Being prepared allows you to anticipate challenges and obstacles that may arise, enabling you to proactively address them before they become insurmountable. For example, a well-prepared project manager anticipates potential risks and develops contingency plans to mitigate them.

2. Increased Efficiency:

Preparation leads to increased efficiency by streamlining processes and eliminating unnecessary steps. For instance, a chef who prepares all ingredients before cooking can complete a recipe more quickly and efficiently.

3. Enhanced Performance:

Preparation enhances performance by allowing you to focus on the task at hand without distractions. Athletes, for example, prepare extensively before competitions to ensure peak performance.

4. Improved Decision-Making:

Being prepared improves decision-making by providing you with the necessary information and time to weigh options and choose the best course of action. A well-prepared business leader makes informed decisions that benefit the organization.

5. Confidence Boost:

Preparation boosts confidence by instilling a sense of readiness and competence. A student who thoroughly prepares for an exam feels more confident and performs better.

6. Time Savings:

Preparation saves time by reducing the need for last-minute scrambling and corrections. For example, a well-prepared speaker delivers a speech more efficiently, saving time and avoiding errors.

7. Stress Reduction:

Being prepared reduces stress by minimizing uncertainties and unexpected situations. A well-prepared traveler, for instance, has all necessary documents and plans in place, reducing travel-related stress.

8. Goal Clarity:

Preparation clarifies goals by helping you understand what needs to be done to achieve them. An entrepreneur who prepares a detailed business plan has a clear roadmap to follow.

9. Resource Optimization:

Preparation optimizes resources by ensuring they are used efficiently and effectively. For example, a well-prepared event planner ensures all resources are allocated appropriately, maximizing the event's success.

10. Adaptability:

Finally, preparation enhances adaptability by equipping you with the tools and mindset to respond to changes and unexpected events. A well-prepared individual can adapt to changing circumstances and seize new opportunities.

In conclusion, preparation is not just a means to an end; it is a fundamental aspect of success in all areas of life. By understanding and embracing the reasons why preparation is crucial, you can unlock your full potential and achieve your goals with confidence and competence.

Reflection Questions: Reasons Why Preparation is Crucial

- ✓ Which of the ten reasons resonates with you the most, and why?
- ✓ How can understanding the importance of preparation help you in setting and achieving your goals?
- ✓ What strategies can you implement to ensure you are consistently prepared in various aspects of your life?

Repercussions of NOT Being Prepared

Preparation is often viewed as a proactive approach to success, but the consequences of not being prepared can be equally profound. In this chapter, we will explore the negative repercussions of being unprepared, highlighting missed opportunities and failures that can result from a lack of preparation.

1. Missed Opportunities:

One of the most significant repercussions of not being prepared is the missed opportunities that result. For example, a salesperson who is unprepared for a client meeting may fail to close a deal, missing out on potential revenue and growth opportunities for their company.

2. Decreased Performance:

Not being prepared can lead to decreased performance in various areas of life. For instance, a student who does not prepare for an exam is likely to perform poorly, affecting their grades and future opportunities.

3. Damaged Reputation:

Lack of preparation can damage your reputation, both personally and professionally. For example, a professional who consistently fails to prepare for meetings may be seen as unreliable and unprofessional by their colleagues and clients.

4. Increased Stress:

Not being prepared can lead to increased stress and anxiety, as you may constantly feel overwhelmed by uncompleted tasks and unmet expectations.

5. Wasted Resources:

Lack of preparation can result in wasted resources, including time, money, and effort. For example, a business that launches a product without proper market research may waste resources on a product that fails to meet customer needs.

6. Poor Decision-Making:

Not being prepared can lead to poor decision-making, as you may make hasty or uninformed decisions without considering all relevant factors.

7. Lost Time:

Lack of preparation can lead to lost time, as you may spend more time correcting mistakes or addressing issues that could have been prevented with proper preparation.

8. Missed Deadlines:

Not being prepared can lead to missed deadlines, which can have serious consequences in both personal and professional settings.

9. Strained Relationships:

Lack of preparation can strain relationships with others, as they may feel frustrated or let down by your lack of readiness.

10. Missed Learning Opportunities:

Finally, not being prepared can result in missed learning opportunities, as you may fail to learn from your experiences and improve your skills and knowledge.

In conclusion, the repercussions of not being prepared can be far-reaching and significant. By understanding these consequences, you can appreciate the importance of preparation in achieving success and avoiding potential pitfalls in your personal and professional life.

Reflection Questions: Repercussions of NOT Being Prepared

- ✓ Think of a time when lack of preparation led to a negative outcome. What did you learn from that experience?
- ✓ How do you think being unprepared affects your ability to capitalize on opportunities?
- ✓ What steps can you take to minimize the negative repercussions of not being prepared in the future?

Why Preparation is Key to One's Success

Success is not a matter of luck or talent alone; it is a result of meticulous preparation and diligent effort. In this chapter, we will examine how preparation leads to success and discuss how preparedness enhances performance and fosters growth.

1. Setting the Stage for Success:

Preparation sets the stage for success by creating a solid foundation upon which to build. Just as a builder prepares the ground before laying the foundation for a building, preparation allows you to create a solid foundation for your success.

2. Enhancing Performance:

Preparedness enhances performance by ensuring that you are ready to perform at your best when the time comes. Athletes, for example, prepare extensively before competitions to ensure that they are in peak condition on the day of the event.

3. Fostering Growth:

Preparation fosters growth by pushing you out of your comfort zone and challenging you to learn and improve. Each time you prepare for a new challenge, you grow and develop new skills and abilities.

4. Maximizing Opportunities:

Preparedness allows you to maximize opportunities that come your way. When you are prepared, you are able to recognize and seize opportunities that others may overlook.

5. Building Confidence:

Preparation builds confidence by giving you the knowledge and skills you need to succeed. When you are well-prepared, you approach challenges with a sense of confidence and assurance.

6. Improving Decision-Making:

Preparedness improves decision-making by providing you with the information and resources you need to make informed choices. When you are well-prepared, you are less likely to make impulsive or uninformed decisions.

7. Overcoming Challenges:

Preparation helps you overcome challenges by giving you the tools and strategies you need to face obstacles head-on. When you are prepared, you are more resilient and better able to handle setbacks.

8. Sustaining Success:

Preparedness is key to sustaining success over the long term. Success is not a one-time event; it is a journey that requires ongoing preparation and effort.

9. Inspiring Others:

Finally, preparation inspires others to follow your lead. When others see the level of preparation and dedication you put into your work, they are inspired to do the same.

In conclusion, preparation is not just a means to an end; it is a fundamental aspect of success. By understanding how preparation leads to success and embracing it as a way of life, you can unlock your full potential and achieve your goals with confidence and determination.

Reflection Questions: Why Preparation is Key to One's Success

- ✓ How do you define success, and how does preparation contribute to it?
- ✓ In what ways can preparation enhance your performance and lead to personal growth?

- ✓ How can you integrate the principle of preparation into your long-term success strategy?

Luck vs. Being Prepared

Luck is often seen by many as a mysterious force that determines success or failure. However, the relationship between that 'so-called' luck and preparation is more nuanced than it may seem. In this chapter, we will explore the concept of this 'so-called' luck and its relationship with preparation, arguing that this 'so-called' luck often favors the prepared.

Understanding Luck:
Luck is often defined as an unpredictable force that brings good or bad fortune. While this 'so-called' luck may play a role in our lives, relying solely on luck is not a sustainable strategy for success.

The Role of Preparation:
Preparation is the key to turning this 'so-called' luck into success. While we cannot control luck, we can control how prepared we are to seize opportunities when they arise.

Luck Favors the Prepared:
The saying *"luck favors the prepared"* highlights the idea that those who are prepared are more likely to recognize and capitalize on opportunities when they arise.

Examples of Luck vs. Being Prepared:
Consider the story of Alexander Fleming, who discovered penicillin by accident. While luck played a role in the discovery, it was Fleming's preparation and scientific knowledge that allowed him to

recognize the significance of the mold that led to the discovery of penicillin.

The Role of Mindset:

The mindset of being prepared can also influence how we perceive and respond to that 'so-called' luck. Those who are prepared are more likely to see opportunities where others see only chance.

Steps to Prepare for Luck:

To prepare for this 'so-called' luck, it is essential to cultivate a mindset of readiness and anticipation. This can be achieved through continuous learning, networking, and staying open to new possibilities.

Action Plan:

- ✓ Identify areas where you want to be successful.
- ✓ Research and learn about those areas to increase your knowledge and expertise.
- ✓ Stay open to new opportunities and be ready to seize them when they arise.
- ✓ Reflect on how preparation has helped you capitalize on opportunities in the past.

In conclusion, while many believe that luck may play a role in their lives, being prepared is the key to turning that 'so-called' luck into success. By cultivating a mindset of readiness and anticipation, we can increase our chances of being in the right place at the right time and seizing opportunities when they arise.

Reflection Questions: Luck vs. Being Prepared

- ✓ Reflect on a time when you attributed success to luck. Could better preparation have played a role?

- ✓ How can you shift your mindset from relying on luck to prioritizing preparation in your endeavors?
- ✓ What practices can you adopt to ensure you are consistently prepared to seize opportunities?

Preparation Can Be Learned

Preparation is not just a natural talent; it is a skill that can be learned and developed over time. In this chapter, we will explore strategies and techniques for developing a habit of preparation, along with stories of individuals who have successfully learned to be prepared.

Understanding the Nature of Preparation:
Preparation is more than just a single act; it is a mindset that involves planning, anticipation, and readiness. By understanding the nature of preparation, we can begin to cultivate it as a habit.

Strategies for Developing a Habit of Preparation:

- ✓ Set clear goals: Define what you want to achieve and create a plan to get there.
- ✓ Break tasks into smaller steps: Break down larger tasks into smaller, more manageable steps to make them easier to prepare for.
- ✓ Use a planner or calendar: Keep track of deadlines and important dates to stay organized and prepared.
- ✓ Practice time management: Learn to prioritize tasks and allocate your time effectively to avoid last-minute rushes.
- ✓ Anticipate obstacles: Identify potential challenges and develop strategies to overcome them before they arise.
- ✓ Learn from past experiences: Reflect on past successes and failures to learn what worked and what didn't in terms of preparation.

Examples of Successful Preparation:
Consider the story of Thomas Edison, who famously said, "Genius is one percent inspiration and ninety-nine percent perspiration." Edison's success was not just the result of his creativity and ingenuity; it was also the result of his meticulous preparation and hard work.

Action Plan:

- ✓ Set a specific goal that requires preparation.
- ✓ Break down the goal into smaller, manageable steps.
- ✓ Create a timeline for each step and set deadlines.
- ✓ Anticipate potential obstacles and develop strategies to overcome them.
- ✓ Reflect on your progress regularly and make adjustments as needed.

In conclusion, preparation is a skill that can be learned and developed with practice. By implementing the strategies outlined in this chapter and learning from the experiences of others, you can cultivate a habit of preparation that will serve you well in all areas of your life.

Reflection Questions: Preparation Can Be Learned

- ✓ What are some skills or habits related to preparation that you would like to develop or improve?
- ✓ How can you create a learning plan to enhance your ability to be prepared in various aspects of your life?
- ✓ What resources or support do you need to effectively learn and practice preparation skills?

How to Be Prepared for Opportunities - Steps with Examples

Opportunities are all around us, but it is our preparedness that allows us to recognize and seize them when they arise. In this chapter, we will offer a step-by-step guide to preparing for opportunities, along with practical examples and scenarios to illustrate each step.

1. Identify Your Goals and Aspirations:

Before you can prepare for opportunities, you must first identify your goals and aspirations. What do you hope to achieve? What opportunities align with your goals?

Example:

Sarah wants to advance her career in marketing and hopes to one day become a marketing manager. She identifies opportunities that will allow her to gain relevant experience and skills in the field.

2. Research and Stay Informed:

Stay informed about trends and developments in your industry or field of interest. Research potential opportunities and understand what they entail.

Example:

John, a software developer, stays updated with the latest technologies and trends in software development. When an opportunity arises to work on a project using a new programming language, he is prepared because he has already familiarized himself with it.

3. Develop Relevant Skills and Expertise:

Identify the skills and expertise required to capitalize on opportunities in your field. Develop these skills through training, education, and practical experience.

Example:
Maria wants to start her own business. She takes courses in entrepreneurship, marketing, and finance to develop the skills she needs to succeed.

4. Build a Strong Network:

Build a network of contacts who can inform you about potential opportunities and provide support and guidance.

Example:
Tom attends networking events and conferences in his industry. Through these connections, he learns about a job opening at a company he admires and is able to secure an interview.

5. Stay Flexible and Open-Minded:

Opportunities may not always come in the form you expect. Stay flexible and open-minded to new possibilities.

Example:
Laura, a graphic designer, is offered an opportunity to work on a project outside her usual scope. Despite initial hesitation, she accepts the challenge and learns new skills that enhance her portfolio.

6. Be Prepared to Take Action:

When an opportunity presents itself, be prepared to take action. Have a plan in place and be ready to execute it.

Example:
When a last-minute speaking opportunity arises at a conference, David, a public speaker, is prepared with a well-rehearsed presentation and seizes the opportunity to showcase his skills.

Action Plan:

- ✓ Identify your goals and aspirations.

- ✓ Research and stay informed about potential opportunities.
- ✓ Develop relevant skills and expertise.
- ✓ Build a strong network of contacts.
- ✓ Stay flexible and open-minded.
- ✓ Be prepared to take action when opportunities arise.

By following these steps and examples, you can be better prepared to recognize and seize opportunities that come your way. Preparation is the key to turning potential opportunities into successful endeavors.
Reflection Questions: How to Be Prepared for Opportunities - Steps with Examples

- ✓ What steps can you take to proactively identify and prepare for potential opportunities?
- ✓ How can you tailor your preparation efforts to align with your personal and professional goals?
- ✓ How will you know when you are adequately prepared to seize an opportunity?

Various Important Examples of Preparation in Life

Preparation is a key factor in achieving success and overcoming challenges in various aspects of life. In this chapter, we will explore different scenarios where preparation is crucial, including business, winning bids, presentations, family, finance, interviews, negotiations, and more. Each scenario will be accompanied by detailed examples and case studies to illustrate the importance of preparation.

1. Business:

Preparation in business is essential for setting goals, developing strategies, and anticipating challenges. For example, a business owner who prepares a comprehensive business plan is more likely to succeed than one who does not.

Example:

Before launching her new business, Sarah conducts thorough market research, prepares a detailed business plan, and develops a marketing strategy to reach her target audience. As a result, her business experiences rapid growth and success.

2. Winning Bids:

Preparation is key when bidding for projects or contracts. Those who prepare thoroughly are more likely to submit competitive bids and win lucrative contracts.

Example:

John, a construction contractor, prepares a detailed bid proposal for a major construction project. He conducts site visits, analyzes project requirements, and submits a bid that is both competitive and comprehensive. As a result, he wins the contract and completes the project successfully.

3. Presentations:

Preparation is crucial for delivering effective presentations that inform, persuade, and engage the audience. Those who prepare well are more likely to deliver memorable and impactful presentations.

Example:

Mary prepares extensively for her upcoming presentation to investors. She rehearses her speech, creates visually appealing slides, and anticipates potential questions. As a result, her presentation is well-received, and she secures the funding she needs for her project.

4. Family:

Preparation is important in family life for planning and organizing activities, managing finances, and ensuring the well-being of family members.

Example:

The Smith family prepares a budget at the beginning of each month to track their expenses and savings. By planning ahead, they are able to avoid financial stress and achieve their financial goals.

5. Finance:

Preparation in financial matters is crucial for managing income, expenses, investments, and savings effectively.

Example:

Tom prepares for his retirement by regularly contributing to his retirement savings account and diversifying his investments. When he retires, he is financially secure and able to enjoy his retirement years comfortably.

6. Interviews:

Preparation is essential for job interviews to showcase your skills, experience, and qualifications effectively.
Example:
Lisa prepares for her job interview by researching the company, practicing common interview questions, and preparing examples of her past accomplishments. As a result, she impresses the interviewers and lands the job.

7. Negotiations:
Preparation is key in negotiations to understand the needs and priorities of both parties and reach a mutually beneficial agreement.
Example:
Mark prepares for a salary negotiation by researching salary ranges for his position, considering his skills and experience. He also identifies his desired salary and benefits package. As a result, he negotiates a salary increase and additional benefits successfully.

These examples illustrate the importance of preparation in various aspects of life. By preparing thoroughly, you can increase your chances of success and achieve your goals more effectively in all areas of life.
Reflection Questions: Various Important Examples of Preparation in Life

- ✓ Consider the various aspects of life mentioned in this chapter. In which areas do you feel most prepared, and in which areas do you see room for improvement?
- ✓ How can you apply the examples of preparation in business, winning bids,

presentations, family, finance, interviews, negotiations, etc., to your own life?

- ✓ What specific actions can you take to better prepare in the areas where you see room for improvement?

Real-life Case Studies of Various Examples of Preparation

Real-life stories of individuals or organizations that have achieved success through preparation serve as powerful examples of the importance of being prepared. In this chapter, we will present several case studies and analyze the strategies and techniques they used to prepare effectively.

Case Study 1: Amazon

Background:

Amazon started as an online bookstore in 1994 and has since grown into one of the largest e-commerce companies in the world.

Preparation Strategy:

Amazon's founder, Jeff Bezos, had a long-term vision for the company and prepared meticulously for its growth. He focused on customer satisfaction, innovation, and long-term planning.

Result:

Amazon's commitment to preparation and long-term planning has paid off, and the company is now a leader in the e-commerce industry, offering a wide range of products and services.

Case Study 2: Elon Musk

Background:

Elon Musk is the founder and CEO of SpaceX, Tesla, and other innovative companies.

Preparation Strategy:

Musk is known for his meticulous preparation and attention to detail. He focuses on developing

groundbreaking technologies and preparing for the future of space exploration and sustainable energy.
Result:
Musk's commitment to preparation has led to numerous successful ventures, including the development of the Falcon rocket and the Tesla electric car.

Case Study 3: Serena Williams
Background:
Serena Williams is one of the most successful tennis players of all time.
Preparation Strategy:
Williams is known for her intense preparation and training regimen. She focuses on physical fitness, mental toughness, and strategic planning for each match.
Result:
Williams' preparation has led to numerous Grand Slam titles and a reputation as one of the greatest athletes in tennis history.

Case Study 4: Steve Jobs
Background:
Steve Jobs was the co-founder and CEO of Apple Inc.
Preparation Strategy:
Jobs was known for his meticulous attention to detail and his focus on creating innovative products that would change the world.
Result:
Jobs' preparation and vision led to the development of groundbreaking products such as the iPhone, iPad, and MacBook, which revolutionized the technology industry.

These case studies highlight the importance of preparation in achieving success. Whether in business, sports, or technology, preparation is often the key to achieving your goals and realizing your dreams.

Reflection Questions: Real-life Case Studies of Various Examples of Preparation

- ✓ Reflect on the case studies presented in this chapter. Which one resonated with you the most, and why?
- ✓ How do these real-life examples inspire you to improve your own preparedness?
- ✓ What specific strategies or approaches from the case studies can you implement in your own life to enhance your preparation?

Embracing Change through Preparedness

In today's rapidly evolving world, change is inevitable. Whether it's in our personal lives or professional endeavors, being prepared for change can make a significant difference in how we adapt and thrive. This chapter explores the importance of embracing change and how preparedness can help us navigate through uncertain times.

The Nature of Change: Change is constant and can manifest in various forms, such as technological advancements, market shifts, or personal circumstances. Understanding the nature of change is the first step toward preparing for it effectively.

The Benefits of Embracing Change: Embracing change opens up new opportunities for growth, innovation, and personal development. It allows us to stay relevant, competitive, and resilient in the face of challenges.

Strategies for Embracing Change:

- ✓ **Continuous Learning:** Stay updated with the latest trends and developments in your field through ongoing learning and professional development.
- ✓ **Flexibility:** Cultivate a mindset of adaptability and flexibility to embrace new ideas and ways of working.
- ✓ **Networking:** Build a strong network of contacts who can provide support and guidance during times of change.

- ✓ **Resilience:** Develop resilience to bounce back from setbacks and see change as an opportunity for growth.
- ✓ **Scenario Planning:** Anticipate potential changes and develop contingency plans to mitigate risks.

Case Studies:

- ✓ **Netflix:** Initially a DVD rental service, Netflix embraced the change to online streaming, revolutionizing the entertainment industry.
- ✓ **Apple:** Under Steve Jobs' leadership, Apple embraced change by introducing innovative products like the iPhone, iPad, and MacBook, setting new standards in technology.

Action Plan:

- ✓ **Assess Your Readiness:** Evaluate your current readiness and willingness to embrace change.
- ✓ **Identify Areas for Improvement:** Identify areas where you can improve your preparedness for change.
- ✓ **Set Goals:** Set specific, achievable goals for embracing change and track your progress.
- ✓ **Seek Feedback:** Solicit feedback from mentors or peers on ways to enhance your readiness for change.

Embracing change is not always easy, but by being prepared and adopting a positive mindset, we can turn change into an opportunity for growth and success.
Reflection Questions: Embracing Change through Preparedness:

- ✓ How has being prepared helped you navigate unexpected changes or challenges in the past?
- ✓ In what areas of your life do you feel least prepared for change, and how can you improve your preparedness in those areas?
- ✓ What steps can you take to build resilience and embrace change through preparedness in your personal and professional life?

Building Resilience Through Preparation

Resilience is the ability to adapt and bounce back from adversity. In today's fast-paced and unpredictable world, building resilience is essential for navigating challenges and achieving success. This chapter explores how preparation can help build resilience and enhance our ability to thrive in the face of adversity.

Understanding Resilience: Resilience is not a fixed trait but a skill that can be developed and strengthened over time. It involves having a positive mindset, strong problem-solving skills, and the ability to manage stress effectively.

The Role of Preparation in Building Resilience: Preparation plays a crucial role in building resilience by:

- ✓ **Anticipating Challenges:** By being prepared, we can anticipate potential challenges and develop strategies to overcome them.
- ✓ **Building Confidence:** Preparation builds confidence, which is essential for facing challenges with a positive attitude.
- ✓ **Enhancing Adaptability:** Preparedness enhances our ability to adapt to new situations and changes, making us more resilient.
- ✓ **Reducing Stress:** Knowing that we are prepared can reduce stress and anxiety, allowing us to respond more effectively to challenges.

Strategies for Building Resilience Through Preparation:

- ✓ **Developing a Growth Mindset:** Embrace challenges as opportunities for growth and learning.
- ✓ **Setting Realistic Goals:** Set achievable goals and develop a plan to reach them.
- ✓ **Cultivating Social Support:** Build a strong support network of friends, family, and colleagues.
- ✓ **Practicing Self-Care:** Take care of your physical and mental well-being through regular exercise, healthy eating, and stress-reducing activities.
- ✓ **Learning from Failure:** View failure as a learning experience and an opportunity to improve.

Case Studies:

- ✓ **Elon Musk:** Despite facing numerous setbacks in his entrepreneurial ventures, Musk's resilience and preparedness have enabled him to achieve success with companies like SpaceX and Tesla.
- ✓ **J.K. Rowling:** Rowling faced rejection from multiple publishers before finding success with the Harry Potter series. Her resilience and determination to succeed ultimately led to her becoming one of the best-selling authors of all time.

Action Plan:

- ✓ **Assess Your Resilience:** Evaluate your current level of resilience and identify areas for improvement.

- ✓ **Develop a Resilience Plan:** Create a plan to enhance your resilience through preparation, setting goals, and seeking support.
- ✓ **Practice Resilience-Building Activities:** Engage in activities that promote resilience, such as mindfulness, journaling, or seeking feedback.

Building resilience through preparation is a lifelong process that requires commitment and effort. By incorporating preparation into our lives, we can enhance our ability to adapt to challenges, overcome obstacles, and achieve our goals.

Reflection Questions: Building Resilience Through Preparation:

- ✓ Reflect on a time when you faced a significant challenge. How did your level of preparedness impact your ability to overcome that challenge?
- ✓ In what ways can you enhance your preparedness to become more resilient in the face of adversity?
- ✓ How can you integrate the principles of preparation and resilience into your daily life to better cope with unexpected events and setbacks?

Avoiding Over-Preparing

While preparation is crucial for success, there is a fine line between being prepared and over-preparing. In this chapter, we will discuss the pitfalls of over-preparing and provide tips on how to strike a balance, ensuring efficient preparation without excessive stress or time investment.

Understanding Over-Preparing:
Over-preparing occurs when you invest more time, energy, and resources into preparation than is necessary or productive. This can lead to burnout, stress, and diminishing returns on your efforts.

Pitfalls of Over-Preparing:

- ✓ Diminished Returns: Spending excessive time on preparation may not significantly improve your outcomes.
- ✓ Increased Stress: Over-preparing can lead to increased stress and anxiety, especially if you feel that your efforts are not yielding the desired results.
- ✓ Missed Opportunities: Focusing too much on preparation can cause you to miss out on valuable opportunities that require immediate action.
- ✓ Perfectionism: Over-preparing can stem from a desire for perfection, which can be detrimental to your mental health and well-being.

Striking a Balance:

- ✓ Set Clear Goals: Define your goals and objectives for preparation to ensure that you are focused and efficient in your efforts.
- ✓ Prioritize Tasks: Identify the most important tasks and focus your preparation efforts on those areas that will have the greatest impact.
- ✓ Set Time Limits: Allocate a specific amount of time for preparation and stick to it to avoid over-investing time in non-essential tasks.
- ✓ Learn to Delegate: Delegate tasks that can be handled by others, allowing you to focus on more critical aspects of preparation.
- ✓ Embrace Imperfection: Accept that perfection is not always attainable and that it is okay to make mistakes or not have all the answers.

Tips for Efficient Preparation:

- ✓ Use Templates and Tools: Utilize templates and tools to streamline your preparation process and save time.
- ✓ Focus on High-Impact Activities: Identify activities that will have the greatest impact on your outcomes and prioritize those tasks.
- ✓ Stay Organized: Keep track of your preparation efforts and progress to avoid duplication of work or missed opportunities.
- ✓ Take Breaks: Allow yourself to take breaks and recharge to avoid burnout and maintain productivity.

Action Plan:

- ✓ Identify areas where you tend to over-prepare.
- ✓ Set clear goals and objectives for your preparation efforts.

- ✓ Prioritize tasks based on their impact and importance.
- ✓ Allocate a specific amount of time for preparation and stick to it.
- ✓ Reflect on your preparation process and make adjustments as needed to avoid over-preparing in the future.

By understanding the pitfalls of over-preparing and implementing strategies to strike a balance, you can ensure that your preparation efforts are efficient, effective, and sustainable in the long run.

Reflection Questions: Avoiding Over-Preparing

- ✓ Reflect on a time when you felt you were over-preparing for a task or opportunity. What were the signs that you were over-preparing?
- ✓ How can you distinguish between thorough preparation and excessive preparation in your daily life?
- ✓ What strategies can you implement to strike a balance between being prepared and avoiding over-preparing in the future?

Preparation Checklist

This checklist is designed to help you assess your preparedness in various aspects of life and serve as a practical tool for implementing the principles discussed in this book. Use it as a guide to ensure you are well-prepared to seize opportunities and overcome challenges.

Personal Preparation:

Health and Wellness:

- ✓ Have you prioritized your physical and mental health?
- ✓ Are you engaging in regular exercise and maintaining a balanced diet?
- ✓ Have you sought professional help when needed?

Personal Development:

- ✓ Do you have a plan for continuous learning and growth?
- ✓ Are you actively seeking opportunities for self-improvement?
- ✓ Have you identified areas for improvement and set specific goals?

Financial Preparedness:

- ✓ Do you have a budget and financial plan in place?
- ✓ Have you set aside emergency savings?
- ✓ Are you investing in your financial future?

Professional Preparation:

Career Development:

- ✓ Have you identified your career goals and aspirations?

- ✓ Are you updating your skills and knowledge to stay relevant in your field?
- ✓ Do you have a plan for advancing your career?

Networking:

- ✓ Are you building and maintaining professional relationships?
- ✓ Do you actively seek out networking opportunities?
- ✓ Have you established a strong professional network?

Goal Setting:

- ✓ Have you set clear, achievable goals for your professional growth?
- ✓ Do you review and adjust your goals regularly?
- ✓ Are your goals aligned with your long-term aspirations?

Preparation for Opportunities:

Opportunity Awareness:

- ✓ Are you open to new opportunities and experiences?
- ✓ Do you actively seek out opportunities for growth and advancement?
- ✓ Are you prepared to seize opportunities when they arise?

Risk Management:

- ✓ Have you identified potential risks and challenges in your personal and professional life?
- ✓ Do you have contingency plans in place to mitigate these risks?
- ✓ Are you prepared to adapt to unexpected changes?

Action Plan:

Implementation Strategy:

- ✓ Review the checklist and identify areas where you need to improve your preparedness.
- ✓ Set specific, measurable goals for improvement in each area.
- ✓ Develop a timeline and action plan for achieving your goals.

Monitoring and Review:

- ✓ Regularly review your progress against your goals.
- ✓ Adjust your action plan as needed to stay on track.
- ✓ Celebrate your successes and learn from your challenges.

Ready Template You Could Use

Use the following template to assess your preparedness in each area:

Area of Assessment:

- ☐ Health and Wellness
- ☐ Personal Development
- ☐ Financial Preparedness
- ☐ Career Development
- ☐ Networking
- ☐ Goal Setting
- ☐ Opportunity Awareness
- ☐ Risk Management

Current Status:

- ☐ Needs Improvement
- ☐ Making Progress
- ☐ Well-Prepared

Action Plan:

- ☐ Identify specific goals for improvement.
- ☐ Develop a timeline and action plan.
- ☐ Monitor progress and adjust as needed.

Reflections:

- ☐ Celebrate successes.
- ☐ Learn from challenges.
- ☐ Continue to strive for improvement.

Quotes by Notable/Famous Personalities on Being Prepared

Quotes have the power to inspire and motivate us to action. In this chapter, we will explore a number of quotes by notable and famous personalities that emphasize the importance of preparation. Each quote will be accompanied by a brief explanation or example to illustrate its significance.

1. *"By failing to prepare, you are preparing to fail."* - Benjamin Franklin
   Explanation: Franklin's quote underscores the importance of preparation in achieving success. Without adequate preparation, failure is more likely.
2. *"Success depends upon previous preparation, and without such preparation, there is sure to be failure."* - Confucius
   Explanation: Confucius emphasizes the role of preparation in achieving success, suggesting that success is the result of careful planning and preparation.
3. *"The will to win is important, but the will to prepare is vital."* - Joe Paterno
   Explanation: Paterno highlights the importance of preparation in sports and life, suggesting that success is not just about wanting to win but also about preparing diligently.
4. *"Give me six hours to chop down a tree and I will spend the first four sharpening the axe."* - Abraham Lincoln

Explanation: Lincoln's quote emphasizes the value of preparation. By sharpening the axe before chopping the tree, Lincoln suggests that preparation is essential for efficiency and success.

5. "*Success is where preparation and opportunity meet.*" - Bobby Unser
   Explanation: Unser's quote suggests that success is the result of being prepared when opportunity arises. Without preparation, opportunities may be missed.
6. *"The best preparation for tomorrow is doing your best today."* - H. Jackson Brown Jr.
   Explanation: Brown Jr. emphasizes the importance of continuous preparation. By doing your best today, you prepare yourself for future success.
7. *"You can't plan for everything or you never get started in the first place."* - Jim Butcher
   Explanation: Butcher's quote acknowledges the balance between preparation and action. While preparation is important, it should not prevent you from taking action.
8. *"By failing to prepare, you are preparing to fail."* - John Wooden
   Explanation: Wooden's quote echoes Benjamin Franklin's sentiment, emphasizing the consequences of not being prepared.
9. *"The more you sweat in peace, the less you bleed in war."* - Norman Schwarzkopf
   Explanation: Schwarzkopf's quote highlights the importance of preparation in military strategy. By preparing diligently during peacetime, one can minimize casualties during war.

10. *"Success is 20% skills and 80% strategy. You might know how to succeed, but more importantly, what's your plan to succeed?"* - Jim Rohn
    Explanation: Rohn emphasizes the importance of having a plan for success. Skills are important, but without a strategy, success is less likely.
11. *"Expect the best. Prepare for the worst. Capitalize on what comes."* - Zig Ziglar
    Explanation: Ziglar's quote suggests a balanced approach to preparation. While expecting the best, it is also important to prepare for the worst and be ready to capitalize on opportunities.
12. *"Before anything else, preparation is the key to success."* - Alexander Graham Bell
    Explanation: Bell's quote emphasizes that preparation should be the first step in any endeavor, as it lays the foundation for success.
13. *"The secret of success in life is for a man to be ready for his opportunity when it comes."* - Benjamin Disraeli
    Explanation: Disraeli's quote underscores the importance of being prepared for opportunities, as success often depends on being ready to seize them.
14. *"Luck is what happens when preparation meets opportunity."* - Seneca
    Explanation: Seneca's quote suggests that luck is not random but the result of being prepared when opportunity arises.

15. *"Success is the result of perfection, hard work, learning from failure, loyalty, and persistence."* - Colin Powell
    Explanation: Powell's quote emphasizes that success is not just about preparation but also about hard work, learning from failure, and persistence.
16. *"Success is no accident. It is hard work, perseverance, learning, studying, sacrifice, and most of all, love of what you are doing or learning to do."* - Pele
    Explanation: Pele's quote highlights that success is the result of various factors, including preparation, hard work, and passion for what you do.
17. *"Plans are nothing; planning is everything."* - Dwight D. Eisenhower
    Explanation: Eisenhower's quote suggests that while plans may change, the process of planning is essential for success.
18. *"The time to repair the roof is when the sun is shining."* - John F. Kennedy
    Explanation: Kennedy's quote emphasizes the importance of preparation and taking action before problems arise.
19. *"It is better to look ahead and prepare than to look back and regret."* - Jackie Joyner-Kersee
    Explanation: Joyner-Kersee's quote suggests that preparation is essential for avoiding regrets in the future.
20. *"Success is not the result of spontaneous combustion. You must set yourself on fire."* - Arnold H. Glasow

Explanation: Glasow's quote emphasizes the need for proactive preparation and action to achieve success.

21. *"The future depends on what you do today."* - Mahatma Gandhi
    Explanation: Gandhi's quote underscores the importance of preparation and action in shaping the future.
22. *"Spectacular achievement is always preceded by unspectacular preparation."* - Robert H. Schuller
    Explanation: Schuller's quote suggests that success is the result of diligent preparation, even if it may not be immediately visible.
23. *"Luck is preparation meeting opportunity."* - Oprah Winfrey
    Explanation: Winfrey's quote echoes the sentiment that luck is not random but the result of being prepared for opportunities.
24. *"The will to succeed is important, but what's more important is the will to prepare."* - Bobby Knight
    Explanation: Knight emphasizes that while the desire to succeed is important, preparation is the key to turning that desire into reality.
25. *"Prepare for the unknown by studying how others in the past have coped with the unforeseeable and the unpredictable."* - George S. Patton
    Explanation: Patton's quote suggests that one way to prepare for the unknown is to study history and learn from the experiences of others.
26. *"It is a rough road that leads to the heights of greatness."* - Seneca

Explanation: Seneca's quote reminds us that the path to success is not easy and requires careful preparation and perseverance.

27. *"The more you sweat in training, the less you bleed in battle."* - Richard Marcinko

    Explanation: This quote highlights the importance of preparation and training in reducing the risks and challenges we face in life.

28. *"Preparation is not the enemy of success, but a prerequisite for it."* - Unknown

    Explanation: This quote challenges the notion that preparation hinders success and instead suggests that it is essential for achieving success.

29. *"It's not the will to win that matters... Everyone has that. It's the will to prepare to win that matters."* - Paul "Bear" Bryant

    Explanation: Bryant's quote highlights the importance of preparation in sports and in life.

30. *"It is not the strongest of the species that survive, nor the most intelligent, but the one most responsive to change."* - Charles Darwin

    Explanation: Darwin's quote highlights the importance of being prepared to adapt to changing circumstances.

31. *"In preparing for battle I have always found that plans are useless, but planning is indispensable."* - Dwight D. Eisenhower

    Explanation: Eisenhower's quote suggests that while plans may change, the act of planning is essential for success.

32. *"Expect the best, plan for the worst, and prepare to be surprised."* - Denis Waitley

Explanation: Waitley's quote encourages us to be prepared for various outcomes, including unexpected ones.

33. *"You don't have to get ready if you stay ready."* - Will Smith

    Explanation: This quote emphasizes the importance of being prepared at all times, so you are ready to seize opportunities when they arise.

The Journey Forward!

In **'Being Prepared: The Key to Unlocking Success** *(The Importance of Preparation to Seize Opportunities)* we have explored the critical role that preparation plays in achieving success in both personal and professional endeavors. Through a comprehensive examination of various aspects of preparation, we have learned valuable lessons from real-life examples, expert insights, and inspirational quotes. As we conclude this journey, let us recap the key points and encourage readers to embrace preparation as a tool for success.

Summary of Key Points:

- ✓ Preparation sets the foundation for success by enabling us to anticipate challenges, make informed decisions, and seize opportunities.
- ✓ Being prepared increases our confidence, improves our decision-making abilities, and enhances our chances of achieving our goals.
- ✓ While preparation is crucial, it is essential to strike a balance and avoid over-preparing, which can lead to stress and inefficiency.
- ✓ Preparation is a lifelong process that requires continuous learning, adaptation, and improvement.

Embracing Preparation for Success:
As we reflect on the insights shared in this book, let us remember that preparation is not just about planning for specific events or situations but about developing a mindset and lifestyle that prioritizes readiness and resilience. By embracing preparation,

we can navigate life's challenges with confidence and seize opportunities for growth and success.

Action Plan:

- ✓ Reflect on your current approach to preparation and identify areas for improvement.
- ✓ Set specific, achievable goals for enhancing your preparation skills in various aspects of your life.
- ✓ Create a personal development plan that includes strategies for continuous learning and growth.
- ✓ Surround yourself with positive influences and seek mentorship from those who exemplify the value of preparation.

Final Thoughts:

As you embark on your journey to embrace preparation, remember that success is not just about achieving your goals but about the person you become in the process. By prioritizing preparation, you are investing in your future self and laying the groundwork for a fulfilling and successful life.

In closing, I encourage you to embrace preparation as a lifelong companion on your journey to success. May you approach each day with a mindset of readiness and resilience, knowing that you are well-prepared to seize opportunities and overcome challenges.

About the Author 'GERARD ASSEY'

Gerard Assey is a Graduate in Economics, a PGD in Management (HRD) and holds a Doctorate in Leadership. Gerard holds several International Qualifications in Sales, Debt Collection, Training & Teaching, and is a 'Fellow' of the prestigious 'Institute of Sales & Marketing Management'-UK, a Certified NLP Practitioner, a 'Certified Trainer', an 'Accredited Management Teacher-Behavioral Sciences', a 'Certified Competency Facilitator', a 'Certified Management Consultant'- (the International credentials of a professional management consultant, awarded in accordance with global standards of the ICMCI); and a Certification from the University of Michigan in 'Successful Negotiation: Essential Strategies and Skills'

He is also a Member of the 'National Association of Sales Professionals' backed with several years experience in varied industries, both in India and Overseas. He also holds an 'Etiquette Consultant' Certification from the USA (by Sue Fox, Author of Best Seller: 'Business Etiquette for Dummies'. She has trained some of the top celebrities' world over). He was also a recipient of a scholarship for extensive training in Japan on 'Corporate Management for India'.

Gerard Assey is 'Founder & Chief Corporate Trainer' of the Group: '**Citius, Altius, Fortius Unlimited**'- an organization that **celebrated 20 years of Glorious Service** in 2021, focusing on 3 Core Competencies:

People. Performance. Profit; in functional areas of Sales & Marketing, HR & Organizational Development, covering Recruitment, Training & Consultancy!

Having managed organizations with large Sales Forces in India & Overseas, his specialization cover extensive areas of Sales Training (All levels - Presentation, Negotiation, Key/ Strategic Accounts Management & Managerial Skills for all sectors), Bid Proposal/ Capture Planning/ Management Trainings, Retail Sales, Customer Service & Customer Retention Programs, Training for Prevention & Collection of Debt, Self & Personal Development Programs (Time Management, Teamwork & Team Building, Business Etiquette & Personal Grooming, Leadership & Managerial Skills, People Management Skills, Train-the-Trainer etc), including preparation of Custom-designed Business Manuals for Internal (HR, Induction, and Sales etc) & External use (Instruction, User Manuals).

Gerard has successfully conducted over 6100 Trainings & Workshops (as of Mar '24) all across India, Middle East, Africa, Europe & S.E. Asia. Besides public programs conducted regularly, both in India & Overseas, he has some of the top names as clients whom he services from Single Owners to large Public & Government undertakings, covering all sectors, for their in-house needs.

His website: www.CollectionSkills.com is the only one in this part of the world to be featured in the 'Collections & Credit Risk Magazine-USA' under 'Who's Who in Training' and ranks TOP, along with other websites listed below on most search engines.

Gerard is author of 117 books already (Mar 2024)

A few of our business related books:

1. Bite-sized Bits on Commonsense Management
2. Heart to Heart on Life's Principles'
3. How to become a Successful Manager
4. The Sales Professionals' Master Workbook of S.Y.S.T.E.M.S
5. The Professional Business Email Etiquette Handbook & Guide
6. The Professional Business Video-Conferencing Etiquette Handbook & Guide
7. Professional Presentation Skills
8. Exceptional Customer Service
9. Professional Tele-Marketing Skills
10. Professional Debt Collection Skills
11. The G.R.E.A.T. Sales & Service Workbook
12. Sales Training Advantage for Results (*The Ultimate Sales Training Manual to enable you stand out as a S.T.A.R.*)
13. CEO Daily Planner & Organizer
14. The Sales Professionals' Master Daily Planner
15. The Professional Debt Collector's Master Daily Planner
16. My Daily Planner & Organizer
17. MY EMERGENCY INFORMATION RECORD (Family Emergency & Peace of Mind Planner)
18. The Ultimate Therapist & Counselors Planner and Organizer
19. Building an Ethical Workplace
20. Managing Relationships at Work
21. Managing Business Meetings Effectively
22. Effective Delegation Skills
23. Goal Setting for Success
24. B2B Selling by Email
25. Professional Business Etiquette & Grooming
26. Dining Etiquette & Table Manners
27. Effective Networking Skills
28. Grooming, Etiquette & Manners for Teens, Young Adults & Future Leaders
29. Inter-Personal Skills
30. Get Ready, Get Hired!
31. Selling in a Recession
32. Effective Receivables Management in an Economic Downturn!
33. Real Estate & Property Sales Training

34. Credit Sales & Accounts Receivable Management
35. Selling Skills for Real Estate & Property Advisors
36. Take G.R.E.A.T. C.A.R.E!
37. Spa, Salon & Health Club Selling Skills
38. Selling Travel, Holiday & MICE Services
39. Selling Skills for Spa's, Salons & Health Clubs
40. Retailing in Salons & Spas
41. Selling Holiday, Vacation, Tours & Packages
42. The Power of Sales Referrals
43. Selling Luxury
44. Technical Selling Skills
45. Financial Advisors Sales Training
46. Dealing with Burnout at Work Monopolize Your Markets
47. Selling to Affluent Customers
48. Growing up with Grace
49. Financial Selling Skills
50. *The Effective Manager's Guide: Key Skills to Thrive*
51. From Aspiring to Inspiring: A Guide for New Managers on the Rise
52. The Power of Focus
53. Selling with Integrity: Sell Like Jesus The Perfect Role Model!
54. 31 Habits of Champions: Your 31-Day Journey to Greatness
55. Rejecting Grasshopper Talk: From Grasshopper to Giant-Killer-*Defeating Giants Daily!*
56. Navigate the AI-Powered Future of Bid & Proposals: Up-Skill to Stay Relevant with Alternative Career Paths & Opportunities
57. Hiring Sales Winners
58. Present with Impact
59. Success Unlocked: *Breaking Free from Habits that Hold You Back*
60. Complaints to Cheers, Feedback to Gold: Mastering Complaints Management
61. Thriving Together: *Cultivating Diversity, Equity, and Inclusion*
62. Coaching Skills for Sales Managers
63. Soaring to Success in Business & Leadership: Swifter, Higher, Stronger!
64. From Classroom to Podium: A Student's Guide to Powerful Public Speaking & Presentation Skills

65. Developing Self-Discipline
66. The CEO's 31-Day Power Plan: Unlocking Success through Essential Traits
67. Credibility Matters
68. A Winning Attitude
69. Bid & Proposal Management Using AI
70. Sales Forecasting: A Practical & Proven Guide to Strategic Sales Forecasting
71. Elevate & Energize: *50 Dynamic & Fun Activities for Peak Workplace Morale*
72. 'Sales SOS! Sales on Fire! *30 Days to Conquer Chaos & the Nightmares of Success!'*
73. Mastering Sales Managerial Skills: *Building High-Performing Teams & Driving Exceptional Results*
74. Eagle-Eyed Leadership: Unleashing the Power of 31 Lessons from Eagles
75. The Ultimate Employee Training Guide: *Training Today, Leading Tomorrow*
76. Being More Accountable at Work
77. Creating a Culture of Continuous Improvement
78. Effective Questioning & Listening Skills
79. The Power of Value Selling
80. The Growth Mindset
81. Mastering Professional Help Desk Skills
82. The Power to Lead with Empathy
83. Being Prepared: The Key to Unlocking Success

Besides regularly contributing to business & trade journals, including international ones such as the 'Creative Training Techniques' and the 'Sales News' of the U.S.A, He is also a member of several prestigious bodies & trade associations, having participated in many Conferences & Workshops in India & Overseas.

Prior to his last assignment of leading & managing a large MNC as head, Gerard had a 3-year stint in the Middle East as a Consultant with a leading British Consultancy Firm.

As the past 'Official Country Representative' for the International Business Award- 'THE STEVIES'-(the business world's own Oscar) for about 4 years- he ensured a few Indian companies that qualify for the same every year!

Gerard can be contacted at:

Email: training@Sales-Training.in,training@CollectionSkills.com

Websites:

www.Sales-Training.in
www.EtiquetteWorks.in
www.CollectionSkills.com
www.RetailSalesTraining.in
www.SalesTrainingIndia.com
www.ManualPreparation.com
www.TrainingWithPuppets.com
www.FirstContactAcademy.com
www.SalesAndMarketingRecruiter.com

Our TRAININGS that can help your team

- ✓ **Sales Effectiveness**: Selling Skills for any Sector: Service/ Logistics/ FMCG Realty/ Insurance & Finance/ Media/ SPA's, Health Clubs & Salons/ Key Account Management, Effective Negotiation Skills/ Bid & Proposal Management Skills/ Retail Sales Training: Any Sector (Auto, Jewelry, Clothing, Luxury etc)
- ✓ **Customer Service Skills**-Complaints Handling & Customer Retention
- ✓ **Debt Prevention & Collection Skills**
- ✓ **Etiquette & Grooming**
- ✓ **Leadership & Managerial Skills**
- ✓ **Self & Personal Development Skills**: Presentation Skills/ Effective Communication Skills/Business Proposal Writing Skills/ Problem Solving & Decision Making Skills/ Empowering Secretaries-The perfect PA! (For Secretaries & PA's)/ Effective Time Management/ Teamwork & Teambuilding/ P.R.I.D.E- **P**ersonal **R**esponsibility **I**n **D**elivering **E**xcellence

www.ingramcontent.com/pod-product-compliance
Lightning Source LLC
LaVergne TN
LVHW010120170826
845678LV00012B/2517

* 9 7 8 8 1 9 7 1 1 2 1 9 5 *